Little RIDDLERS

Hertfordshire Poets

Edited By Daisy Job

First published in Great Britain in 2018 by:

Young Writers
Remus House
Coltsfoot Drive
Peterborough
PE2 9BF
Telephone: 01733 890066
Website: www.youngwriters.co.uk

All Rights Reserved
Book Design by Ashley Janson
© Copyright Contributors 2018
SB ISBN 978-1-78896-624-5
Printed and bound in the UK by BookPrintingUK
Website: www.bookprintinguk.com
YB0364U

FOREWORD

Dear Reader,

Are you ready to get your thinking caps on to puzzle your way through this wonderful collection?

Young Writers' Little Riddlers competition set out to encourage young writers to create their own riddles. Their answers could be whatever or whoever their imaginations desired; from people to places, animals to objects, food to seasons. Riddles are a great way to further the children's use of poetic expression, including onomatopoeia and similes, as well as encourage them to 'think outside the box' by providing clues without giving the answer away immediately.

All of us here at Young Writers believe in the importance of inspiring young children to produce creative writing, including poetry, and we feel that seeing their own riddles in print will keep that creative spirit burning brightly and proudly.

We hope you enjoy riddling your way through this book as much as we enjoyed reading all the entries.

CONTENTS

Cherry Tree Primary School, Watford

Billy Johnson (7)	1
Enakshi Jindal (6)	2
Ammara Shakil (7)	4
Sami Hare (7)	6
Freya Jane Fitzsimmons (7)	7
Areesha Kiani (7)	8
Mia Bond (7)	9
Sarah Khan (6)	10
Qasim Parvaz (7)	11
Drishna Patel (7)	12
Isabella Amber Bruce (7)	13
Nihaal Shivji (6)	14
Alice Juliette Rogers (7)	15
Ted Mckenzie (6)	16
Rudra Desai (7)	17
Nathan Trang (7)	18
Heath Rodingo (7)	19
Savannah Ilawole-Marsh (6)	20
Rish Nathubhai (6)	21
Saaliha Irshad (7)	22
Ghadeer Ali (7)	23
Sophia Mariam Khodabux (6)	24
Adiyan Zaman (7)	25
Scarlett Federico-Harvey (6)	26
Lawrence Ladimeji (6)	27
Ethan Young (7)	28
Mahum Faraz (6)	29
Eyad Butt (6)	30
Isabelle Swinford (7)	31
Jeremiah Bovell (6)	32
Lilia Perretta (7)	33
Ethan Collyer (6)	34
Jude Amoako (7)	35
Bailey Tibbles (6)	36
Khalid Hydara (7)	37

Commonswood Primary School, Welwyn Garden City

Darsi-Bleu King (6)	38
Imogen Turner (5)	39
Ruby Hunt (6)	40
Oliver Dodman (5)	41
Layla Clark (6)	42
Reshai Fox (6)	43
Jude (5)	44
Tyler Gary David Groome (6)	45
Harvey Meager (5)	46
Dora Kancsar (6)	47
Emilia Isavella Coles (6)	48
Manogna Pulatakura (5)	49
Angus Seth Josiah Shields (5)	50
Mia Roberts (6)	51
Maia Ghumania (6)	52
Mahita Pulapakura (5)	53
Aston-Kai Timms (6)	54
Rory Earl Corcoran (6)	55
Bella (5)	56
Lottie Hardy (5)	57
Ava French (6)	58
Lucas Crowley (6)	59
Austin MacDonald (5)	60
Zachary Taylor (5)	61
Evie Ruth Higgins (5)	62
Grace Sparks (5)	63
Bailey (5)	64
Louis Trichardt-Sano (6)	65
Oliver (5)	66
Thomas Andrews (6)	67

Chase Lee Curtis (6)	68
Annierose Bloom (6)	69
Jay Hickson (5)	70
Delara De Graaf (6)	71
Lexi Jo Hannibal (5)	72

Dewhurst St Mary CE Primary School, Cheshunt

Amelie Cording (6)	73
Eleana Hajdarmataj (6)	74
Millie Taylor (6)	75
Amber-Moné Brown (6)	76
Skye Norton (6)	77
Papa Gyamfi Osei Afriyie (6)	78
Sonny-Charles Lewis (6)	79

St Albans High School For Girls Primary School, Wheathampstead

Mabel Gleeson (5)	80
Emilia Calleja (5)	81
Ava Harding (6)	82
Melissa Wang (6)	83
Diya Thusu (5)	84
Marie Elena Zu Dohna (6)	85
Natasha Gilbert (5)	86
Aarya Vimal Raval (6)	87
Anna Lucia Gonzalez (5)	88
Sarah Elizabeth Hallas (6)	89
Lara Ghosh (5)	90
Freya Burner (6)	91

St Mary's CE Academy, Hitchin

Stanley Webb (7)	92
Hannah Crone (7)	93
Sophie Ruby Ann Deane (7)	94
Jonathan Saunders (6)	95
Lucas Hall-Watts (7)	96
Isla Lyons (7)	97
Phoeby Drew (6)	98
Sarah Danila (6)	99

Jessica Luisa Terriss (7)	100
Coen Chan (7)	101
Freddie Thomas Martin (7)	102
Zeeva Turner (7)	103
Phoebe Eliza Hooper (7)	104
Bryher Goodluck (6)	105
Ellie Newman (6)	106
Finley Horton (6)	107
London-Grace Isabella Maria Rodrigues de Souza (6)	108
Isabelle Marsh (6)	109
Jamie Thompson (7)	110
Grace Kelly (7)	111
Freya Jane Shapland (7)	112
Miles O'Brien (7)	113
Felix Weston (6)	114
Sid White (6)	115
Toby Matthew Pearce (6)	116
Logan Hall (7)	117
James Lyon (6)	118
Morgan John Geary (7)	119
William Whybrow (6)	120
Blue Bartlett (7)	121
Peyton Jean Day (7)	122
Oliver Ibbotson (7)	123
Eliana Miles (6)	124
Alfie Witherington (6)	125
Max Harvey (6)	126
Liam Maw (7)	127
Connor Crook (6)	128

Trent CE Primary School, Cockfosters

Elysia Kyriacou	129
Paraskevi Angeli (6)	130
Greatwin Anyanwu (6)	131
Ben Jones (7)	132
Isabella Fitzgerald (6)	133
Zoe Koureas (6)	134
Christopher Jacovou (7)	135
Natasha Anna Kyriacou (7)	136

Warren Dell Primary School, South Oxhey

Madeline Valentine (7)	137
Alex Webster (7)	138
Aiva Lardner (7)	139
Alfie Quidder-Hart (7)	140
Jessica Burman (6)	141

THE POEMS

What Am I?

I can weigh between 3-8kg.
I measure approximately 46-68cm.
I am a carnivore, that means I only eat meat.
I eat leftovers from other animals such as the polar bear.
I can run quite fast.
I hunt in big packs to get my prey.
I have thick fur on my tail and it's useful for cover in cold weather.
I eat small animals such as lemmings and voles to keep me alive.
My most distinctive feature is all my whiskers on my head.
I use my thick tail to balance.
What am I?

Answer: An Arctic fox.

Billy Johnson (7)
Cherry Tree Primary School, Watford

What Am I?

My predator is a polar bear.
I am mostly recognised by my sharp, pointy claws.
I am not a mammal and I'm smaller than an Arctic hare.

I have snowy, white fur on my wings.
My coat is furry.
I'm camouflaged by my wings.

I belong to the bird family and live on trees.
I have strong legs and I I sleep in a nest.
My most distinctive feature is my orange beak.

I fly down and hunt for some prey,
when I am hungry,

I glide, I dive and I hunt for the Arctic hare.

What am I?

Answer: A snowy owl.

Enakshi Jindal (6)
Cherry Tree Primary School, Watford

What Am I?

I am most easily recognised by my white fur on my body.
I have snowy fur on my feathers.
My coat is very warm.
I am camouflaged by my long feathers.
I am smaller than a polar bear but larger than an Arctic hare.
I belong to the owl family.
I sleep in a nest.
I have tiny legs and no arms.
My most distinctive feature is my beak.
I use my wings to fly.
When I am hungry, I will search for fish and Arctic hares.

I am a bit like a predator but I am not.
I live in the Arctic.
What am I?

Answer: A snowy owl.

Ammara Shakil (7)
Cherry Tree Primary School, Watford

What Am I?

I have white fur on my body.
My coat is furry.
I am camouflaged by my white fur.
I am smaller than an Arctic wolf but bigger than a lemming.
I have small legs and white fur.
My most distinctive feature is my pure white fur.
I use my white fur to camouflage.
When I am hungry, I will try to find leaves.
I live in the tundra.
I belong to the rabbit family.
I am most recognised by my small ears.
I sleep in a burrow.
What am I?

Answer: An Arctic hare.

Sami Hare (7)
Cherry Tree Primary School, Watford

What Am I?

I weigh over 1700 kilograms.
Did you know, you can tell how old I am from how many rings I have in a cross section of my tooth?
I am the largest fin-footed mammal.
I am a carnivore which means I eat meat.
I have whiskers and scales.
I use my tusks to help me get out of the water.
I also create breathing holes in the ice.
I can walk on my fins.
I will use my tusks to fight and show my dominance.
What am I?

Answer: A walrus.

Freya Jane Fitzsimmons (7)
Cherry Tree Primary School, Watford

What Am I?

I live on the rocky slopes and upland tundra of the Arctic.
I have white fur on my body.
I can run up to forty miles per hour.
I have small ears.
I am smaller than a polar bear.
I am a herbivore.
I have a pure white coat in winter and a brown coat during the summertime.
This helps me keep warm and camouflaged.
It also helps to protect me during both seasons.
What am I?

Answer: An Arctic hare.

Areesha Kiani (7)
Cherry Tree Primary School, Watford

What Am I?

I live in the Arctic where it is cold and snowy.
I have a nice warm coat.
It keeps me warm in the winter.
My tail is round and fluffy.
I am a herbivore which means I eat plants.
If a predator comes, I hide in the snow.
I am really jumpy.
I have a coat that is white in the winter and brown in the summer.
I live on rocky slopes.
My coat is really fluffy.
What am I?

Answer: An Arctic hare.

Mia Bond (7)
Cherry Tree Primary School, Watford

What Am I?

I can weigh between 2.5-5.5 kilograms.
I measure approximately 43-70 centimetres.
I live in a burrow.
In winter, my fur is white and in summer, my fur is brown.
I eat plants like leaves and bushes.
My ears are small to help keep me warm during the cold winters.
I live on the rocky slopes of the upland tundra of the Arctic.
I can run up to forty miles per hour.
What am I?

Answer: An Arctic hare.

Sarah Khan (6)
Cherry Tree Primary School, Watford

What Am I?

I feed on fish and I feed on octopus.
My sharp tusk fights others to eat and survive.
I weigh between 800-1600 kilograms.
I am a mammal.
I am a medium-sized animal with a sharp, long tusk.
I normally swim with groups.
I am a carnivore which means I eat meat.
I have a pointy, long tusk which can measure up to 3.1 metres.
I can live up to fifty years old.
What am I?

Answer: A narwhal.

Qasim Parvaz (7)
Cherry Tree Primary School, Watford

What Am I?

I have silky fur on my body.
My coat is slippery in the water.
I am smaller than a polar bear but bigger than an Arctic hare.
I belong to the pinniped family.
I am a mammal.
I have a tail and flippers.
I am camouflaged when hibernating.
I use my tusks to help me make breathing holes in the ice.
You know that I have grown because my tusks get longer.
What am I?

Answer: A walrus.

Drishna Patel (7)
Cherry Tree Primary School, Watford

What Am I?

I am easily recognised by my black ears.
I am camouflaged by my white fur.
My coat is fluffy and white.
I am smaller than a fierce polar bear.
I have white legs and a pink nose.
I live in a burrow.
I use my teeth to eat.
We catch plants.
We live in a dark, wet and spooky holes.
I am part of the rabbit family.
What am I?

Answer: An Arctic hare.

Isabella Amber Bruce (7)
Cherry Tree Primary School, Watford

What Am I?

I live in the sea.
I eat fish.
I am a carnivore.
I have one tusk for my nose.
I can catch fish with my tusk and eat them.
I can kill people and whales.
I have a small fin.
My tusk is very long and sharp.
I am a sea mammal that breathes out of water.
I can swim slowly in the water.
I can bounce in the water.
What am I?

Answer: A narwhal.

Nihaal Shivji (6)
Cherry Tree Primary School, Watford

What Am I?

I have four legs and four hooves.
My coat is rough.
I am camouflaged by my white, grey and brown fur.
I am smaller than a polar bear but larger than an Arctic hare.
When I am hungry, I will eat grass.
I am easily recognised by my antlers.
I belong to the deer family.
I live in the Arctic.
What am I?

Answer: A reindeer.

Alice Juliette Rogers (7)
Cherry Tree Primary School, Watford

What Am I?

I weigh between 3-8 kilograms.
I measure approximately 46-68 centimetres.
I have a thick, warm coat.
It is brown in the summer and white in the winter.
This means I can stay well camouflaged all year.
Did you know I have a thick tail?
It is very useful as warm cover in cold weather.
What am I?

Answer: An Arctic fox.

Ted Mckenzie (6)
Cherry Tree Primary School, Watford

What Am I?

I am most easily recognised by my colour.
I am smaller than a blue whale but larger than a seal.
I belong to the mammal family.
I have no legs but I have a tail.
I live in the sea.
I use my powerful tail to attack my predators.
I am black and white.
I have a fin on my back.
What am I?

Answer: A killer whale.

Rudra Desai (7)
Cherry Tree Primary School, Watford

What Am I?

I live on the rocky slopes and upland tundra of the Arctic.
I have a pure white coat during the winter and a brown coat during the summertime.
I weigh between 2.5-5 kilograms.
I measure approximately 43-70 centimetres.
My ears are small to help keep me warm during the cold winter.
What am I?

Answer: An Arctic hare.

Nathan Trang (7)
Cherry Tree Primary School, Watford

What Am I?

I have a great sense of smell.
I smell my prey from one metre away.
I weigh between 175-650 kilograms.
I measure approximately 2-3 metres.
I normally hunt in the morning.
I have sharp claws to rip apart my prey.
My paws prevent them from breaking through the ice and snow.
What am I?

Answer: A polar bear.

Heath Rodingo (7)
Cherry Tree Primary School, Watford

What Am I?

I am most easily recognised by my bushy tail.
I have white fur on my body.
My coat is white.
I am camouflaged by the snow.
I am smaller than a polar bear but larger than an ant.
I do not have a fin.
I belong to the rabbit family.
I sleep in a small burrow.
What am I?

Answer: An Arctic hare.

Savannah Ilawole-Marsh (6)
Cherry Tree Primary School, Watford

What Am I?

I eat any small animals such as lemmings or voles.
If food is scarce, I scavenge from animals such as polar bears.
I can weigh between 3-8 kilograms.
I measure approximately 46-68 centimetres.
I have a thick, warm coat which is brown in the summer and white in the winter.
What am I?

Answer: An Arctic fox.

Rish Nathubhai (6)
Cherry Tree Primary School, Watford

What Am I?

I have a great sense of smell.
I can smell seals almost one kilometre away and under one metre of snow.
I weigh between 175-605 kilograms.
I measure approximately 2-3 metres.
I hunt seals so then I will not be hungry.
I have white fur.
I am a carnivore.
What am I?

Answer: A polar bear.

Saaliha Irshad (7)
Cherry Tree Primary School, Watford

What Am I?

Did you know you can tell how old I am by the rings on my two teeth?
Some males can weigh more than 1700 kilograms.
I use my tusks to help me climb.
I am a mammal that swims in the sea.
I am one of the largest mammals in the Arctic.
I go on land as well.
What am I?

Answer: A walrus.

Ghadeer Ali (7)
Cherry Tree Primary School, Watford

What Am I?

I am a sea animal.
I can live up to fifty years old.
I am a carnivore which means I eat fish.
I have a long tusk and I duel in the summer.
I can measure between 3.95-5.5 metres.
I weigh between 800-1600 kilograms.
I poke fish to eat my prey.
What am I?

Answer: A narwhal.

Sophia Mariam Khodabux (6)
Cherry Tree Primary School, Watford

What Am I?

I am fin-footed.
I am one of the largest mammals in the Arctic.
You can tell how old I am by the number of rings in a cross section of my teeth.
I can walk on my hind fins.
My tusks help me climb out of the water.
I weigh over 1700kg.
What am I?

Answer: A walrus.

Adiyan Zaman (7)
Cherry Tree Primary School, Watford

What Am I?

I will eat any small animal such as lemmings and voles.
If food is scarce, I will scavenge leftovers from other animals.
I can weigh between 3-8 kilograms.
I measure approximately 46-68 centimetres.
What am I?

Answer: An Arctic fox.

Scarlett Federico-Harvey (6)
Cherry Tree Primary School, Watford

What Am I?

I live in the Arctic.
I can fly.
I have a beak so I can give food to my babies.
I have claws.
My fur is soft.
I live in my nest.
My beak and claws are sharp.
I have wings to fly.
What am I?

Answer: A snowy owl.

Lawrence Ladimeji (6)
Cherry Tree Primary School, Watford

What Am I?

I have very, very deep feathers.
I can see very far with my eyes.
I am used to the dark.
I eat a lot of food.
I live in a spooky, dark cave.
My favourite foods are worms and ants.
What am I?

Answer: A snowy owl.

Ethan Young (7)
Cherry Tree Primary School, Watford

What Am I?

I live in the snow.
My coat is white.
I live in the Arctic.
I have big claws.
I am big in the Arctic.
I have a big, black nose.
I have a shiny nose.
I have white ears.
What am I?

Answer: A polar bear.

Mahum Faraz (6)
Cherry Tree Primary School, Watford

What Am I?

I am really furry and I like to fly.
Later, I like to search for fish.
I have yellow and black eyes.
I use my black eyes so I can see in the dark.
I also have sharp claws on my feet.
What am I?

Answer: A snowy owl.

Eyad Butt (6)
Cherry Tree Primary School, Watford

What Am I?

I am most easily recognised by my big wings.
My coat is grey and white.
I am camouflaged by my whiteness.
I am smaller than a walrus but bigger than a lemming.
I live in the tundra.
What am I?

Answer: A snowy owl.

Isabelle Swinford (7)
Cherry Tree Primary School, Watford

What Am I?

I am mostly recognised by my large paws.
I am the biggest bear.
I live in a cold cave in the Arctic.
I am the biggest Arctic animal on Earth.
I am a carnivore.
I eat seals.
What am I?

Answer: A polar bear.

Jeremiah Bovell (6)
Cherry Tree Primary School, Watford

What Am I?

I sleep in a cave.
I am a carnivore.
I live in the Arctic.
I eat fish.
I like to swim.
I eat seals.
I have four legs.
I have large paws.
My fur is white.
What am I?

Answer: A polar bear.

Lilia Perretta (7)
Cherry Tree Primary School, Watford

What Am I?

I eat small animals such as voles and lemmings.
If my food escapes, I will eat leftovers from other animals such as polar bears.
I can weigh between 5-8kg.
I measure 46-68cm.
What am I?

Answer: An Arctic fox.

Ethan Collyer (6)
Cherry Tree Primary School, Watford

What Am I?

I live in the Arctic on the rocky slopes.
I can run up to forty miles per hour.
I have a white coat in the winter and a brown coat in the summer.
I have small ears.
What am I?

Answer: An Arctic hare.

Jude Amoako (7)
Cherry Tree Primary School, Watford

What Am I?

I have fluffy fur.
I have small ears.
I live in the fox family.
I eat lemmings and voles.
I howl at night.
I'm a carnivore.
I have a bushy tail.
What am I?

Answer: An Arctic fox.

Bailey Tibbles (6)
Cherry Tree Primary School, Watford

What Am I?

I have sharp claws.
I sleep in a den.
I have sharp teeth.
I kill fish to eat.
I am furry and white.
What am I?

Answer: A polar bear.

Khalid Hydara (7)
Cherry Tree Primary School, Watford

A Jungle Riddle

I can be very colourful.
I can fly in the sky.
I live in the zoo in a tree.
I am very noisy because I copy people.
I eat bird food.
I am as fast as an aeroplane.
I eat lots of food like a gorilla.
I have two eyes and one mouth.
I talk with my mouth by opening and closing it.
What am I?

Answer: A parrot.

Darsi-Bleu King (6)
Commonswood Primary School, Welwyn Garden City

What Am I?

They have four legs.
They have a long neck.
Their necks are as tall as trees.
They are orange with brown patches on their skin.
They are not cheetahs.
They have large blue tongues to eat leaves from the trees.
They have long tails, as long as a skipping rope.
They live in Africa.
What are they?

Answer: Giraffes.

Imogen Turner (5)
Commonswood Primary School, Welwyn Garden City

Jungle Riddles

I am very colourful like a rainbow.
I can fly like a bat.
I am as fast as a helicopter at seventy miles per hour.
I live in the zoo like a barn owl.
I am very noisy like a bird.
I have a beak like a chicken.
I eat birdseed like a bird.
What am I?

Answer: A parrot.

Ruby Hunt (6)
Commonswood Primary School, Welwyn Garden City

A Jungle Riddle

There are lots of types of these.
They can jump as high as a kangaroo.
They have red bottoms, as red as a tomato.
They have white teeth, as white as a polar bear.
They eat bananas all day long.
They look like humans.
What are they?

Answer: Monkeys.

Oliver Dodman (5)
Commonswood Primary School, Welwyn Garden City

Tall Eater

I have eyes as small as a grain of sand.
I have spots on me.
I like green leaves.
I have a very long tongue.
I have a very long neck.
I have a little tail.
I have long legs.
I don't have fur.
What am I?

Answer: A giraffe.

Layla Clark (6)
Commonswood Primary School, Welwyn Garden City

A Jungle Riddle

I am as fast as a car.
I have orange and black stripes.
My tummy is white.
I live in the jungle.
I have whiskers.
I eat meat and I drink water.
I have cubs.
I roar a lot.
I have sharp teeth.
What am I?

Answer: A tiger.

Reshai Fox (6)
Commonswood Primary School, Welwyn Garden City

Rainbow Flyer

I have rainbow wings as colourful as a butterfly.
I have soft feathers.
I live in the leafy trees.
My beak is strong.
I have claws that are pointy.
My small eyes are as black as night.
What am I?

Answer: A parrot.

Jude (5)
Commonswood Primary School, Welwyn Garden City

Top Swinger

I have a really big tail.
I have small eyes.
I have a small nose.
I have really small ears.
I have really long legs with sharp claws.
I have small hands.
I am small like a dog.
What am I?

Answer: A monkey.

Tyler Gary David Groome (6)
Commonswood Primary School, Welwyn Garden City

A Jungle Riddle

I am as stripy as a zebra.
My stripes are orange, black and white.
I have sharp teeth.
I have cubs.
My favourite thing to eat is meat.
I live in the jungle.
I have whiskers.
What am I?

Answer: A tiger.

Harvey Meager (5)
Commonswood Primary School, Welwyn Garden City

Big Hunter

I have sharp claws like needles.
I can live in the zoo or the jungle.
My fur is as soft as a cat.
I have stripes like a zebra.
I am a huge, orange animal.
I am not a kind of pet.
What am I?

Answer: A *tiger*.

Dora Kancsar (6)
Commonswood Primary School, Welwyn Garden City

A Jungle

I have a small tail.
I have cute eyes like a penguin.
I am normally found in a zoo or a jungle.
I eat bananas.
I have brown, furry skin.
I can swing from tree to tree.
What am I?

Answer: A monkey.

Emilia Isavella Coles (6)
Commonswood Primary School, Welwyn Garden City

Top Climber

I have soft, furry skin.
I have a little tail.
I live in the treetops.
My fur is like a soft pillow.
My ears are as black as coal.
You can't keep me as a pet.
What am I?

Answer: A monkey.

Manogna Pulatakura (5)
Commonswood Primary School, Welwyn Garden City

A Jungle Riddle

I am stripy like a zebra.
My stripes are black and orange.
I have sharp claws and teeth.
My favourite thing to eat is meat.
I live in the jungle.
I can swim fast.
What am I?

Answer: A *tiger*.

Angus Seth Josiah Shields (5)
Commonswood Primary School, Welwyn Garden City

What Am I?

I have sharp paws.
I live in the zoo and in the jungle.
My fur is as warm as the sun.
I am not a kind of pet.
My eyes are very small.
I have a long, stripy tail.
What am I?

Answer: A tiger.

Mia Roberts (6)
Commonswood Primary School, Welwyn Garden City

A Jungle Riddle

I am cheeky.
I swing on trees.
I eat bananas.
I have a long tail.
I can do tricks on you.
I can sneak up on you.
My skin is brown.
My tail curls up.
What am I?

Answer: A monkey.

Maia Ghumania (6)
Commonswood Primary School, Welwyn Garden City

What Am I?

I am as tall as a tree.
I have brown spots on my body, neck and head.
I live in the jungle.
Also, I eat leaves.
I have a long neck.
I have a short tail.
What am I?

Answer: A giraffe.

Mahitha Pulapakura (5)
Commonswood Primary School, Welwyn Garden City

What Am I?

I have lots of colours on my feathers.
I copy what you say.
I begin with the letter P.
My feathers are red, blue and yellow.
My claws are as sharp as a spike.
What am I?

Answer: A parrot.

Aston-Kai Timms (6)
Commonswood Primary School, Welwyn Garden City

Man Eater

I am a big cat.
I have fur.
I live in a place where you don't.
I have whiskers that feel like wire.
I am a bit soft.
You can't keep me as a pet.
What am I?

Answer: A tiger.

Rory Earl Corcoran (6)
Commonswood Primary School, Welwyn Garden City

Top Climber

I have soft, furry skin.
I have a little tail.
I live in the treetops.
My fur is like a soft pillow.
My ears are round.
You can't keep me as a pet.
What am I?

Answer: A monkey.

Bella (5)
Commonswood Primary School, Welwyn Garden City

Spotty Animals

I have a long neck, as long as a tree.
My tongue is as long as a snake.
I live in the green jungle.
My fur is cuddly.
I am furry.
I have hooves.
What am I?

Answer: A giraffe.

Lottie Hardy (5)
Commonswood Primary School, Welwyn Garden City

A Jungle Riddle

I have a long neck.
I am as tall as a tree.
I eat the greenest leaves.
I have patterns.
I am brown and yellow.
My tail is as small as a mouse.
What am I?

Answer: A giraffe.

Ava French (6)
Commonswood Primary School, Welwyn Garden City

A Jungle Riddle

I am blue, yellow and red.
I have sharp claws.
I have blue eyes.
I am really noisy.
I live in the jungle.
I have sharp claws like an owl.
What am I?

Answer: A parrot.

Lucas Crowley (6)
Commonswood Primary School, Welwyn Garden City

A Jungle Riddle

I am colourful like a rainbow.
I have a sharp beak like a knife.
I can fly in the sky.
I copy people.
I live in the jungle.
I eat bugs.
What am I?

Answer: A parrot.

Austin MacDonald (5)
Commonswood Primary School, Welwyn Garden City

What Am I?

I copy what you say.
I have sharp claws.
I have a sharp beak.
I am as colourful as a rainbow.
I have wings.
I can fly like an eagle.
What am I?

Answer: A parrot.

Zachary Taylor (5)
Commonswood Primary School, Welwyn Garden City

A Jungle Riddle

I live in the jungle.
I swing in trees.
I have fur and soft skin.
I have a long tail.
I eat bananas.
I am as strong as an elephant.
What am I?

Answer: A monkey.

Evie Ruth Higgins (5)
Commonswood Primary School, Welwyn Garden City

A Jungle Riddle

I am as tall as a tree.
I am tall so I can touch the top of the trees.
I have a long, tall neck.
I eat leaves.
I live in the jungle.
What am I?

Answer: A giraffe.

Grace Sparks (5)
Commonswood Primary School, Welwyn Garden City

Top Climber

I have a long tail.
I have little hands.
I have little eyes like a bird.
I can climb up trees.
I can swim.
I can run fast.
What am I?

Answer: A monkey.

Bailey (5)
Commonswood Primary School, Welwyn Garden City

What Am I?

My name starts with a G.
I eat leaves.
I am as tall as a tree.
I am black and yellow.
I have a thin neck.
I am strong.
What am I?

Answer: A giraffe.

Louis Trichardt-Sano (6)
Commonswood Primary School, Welwyn Garden City

Striped Hunter

I have stripes.
I have eyes as big as a rock.
I have claws as big as a spike.
I have hard whiskers.
I live in the forest.
What am I?

Answer: A tiger.

Oliver (5)
Commonswood Primary School, Welwyn Garden City

What Am I?

I have a beak as yellow as a cheetah.
I have black claws.
I am colourful.
I have sharp claws, as sharp as a lizard.
What am I?

Answer: A parrot.

Thomas Andrews (6)
Commonswood Primary School, Welwyn Garden City

What Am I?

My fur can be black, brown or white.
I have four big paws.
I use them to eat.
I can be fierce.
I can scare you.
What am I?

Answer: A bear.

Chase Lee Curtis (6)
Commonswood Primary School, Welwyn Garden City

What Am I?

I am as stripy as a zebra.
I have sharp teeth.
My legs are as strong as a shark.
My claws are as strong as a whale.
What am I?

Answer: A tiger.

Annierose Bloom (6)
Commonswood Primary School, Welwyn Garden City

A Jungle Riddle

I can fly high and as fast as an aeroplane.
You can have me for a pet.
I copy people.
I am very annoying.
What am I?

Answer: A parrot.

Jay Hickson (5)
Commonswood Primary School, Welwyn Garden City

What Am I?

I am as soft as a bear.
I am scary.
I am not like a dog or a cat.
I am an animal.
What am I?

Answer: A monkey.

Delara De Graaf (6)
Commonswood Primary School, Welwyn Garden City

A Jungle

I sit in the tallest trees.
I can fly as fast as a plane.
I am rainbow-coloured.
What am I?

Answer: A parrot.

Lexi Jo Hannibal (5)
Commonswood Primary School, Welwyn Garden City

What Am I?

I am smaller than a plant.
I am as cute as Amelie's teddy.
I am as fluffy as a teddy bear.
I live in a cage.
I have a wheel in my cage.
I have hay and a drink, also food.
I am a pet.
I have orange, fluffy fur.
I like to crunch on cabbage.
My paws are so small, that's why I walk so slowly.
I like to eat grass and flowers.
I like to eat vegetables.
What am I?

Answer: A guinea pig.

Amelie Cording (6)
Dewhurst St Mary CE Primary School, Cheshunt

What Am I?

I have black and white stripes.
I am an animal.
I live in the zoo.
I can't be kept as a pet.
I have a mane like a lion.
I look like a crossing.
I like to crunch hay.
I am as cute as a bear.
I am friendly.
I have a pink tongue.
What am I?

Answer: A zebra.

Eleana Hajdarmataj (6)
Dewhurst St Mary CE Primary School, Cheshunt

What Am I?

I am spotty.
I am yellow and orange.
My fur is as soft as a teddy bear.
I like to crunch leaves.
I have a very long neck.
I have a blue tongue.
I live in the zoo in Africa.
What am I?

Answer: A giraffe.

Millie Taylor (6)
Dewhurst St Mary CE Primary School, Cheshunt

What Am I?

I'm spotty.
I am not a leopard.
I live in the jungle.
I can run very fast.
I can't be a pet.
I can scare you in the jungle.
I am friendly to others.
What am I?

Answer: A cheetah.

Amber-Moné Brown (6)
Dewhurst St Mary CE Primary School, Cheshunt

What Am I?

I am smaller than my friend Skye.
I have two big, floppy ears.
I eat carrots.
I come out at Easter.
I am as cute as a flower.
I enjoy jumping high.
What am I?

Answer: A rabbit.

Skye Norton (6)
Dewhurst St Mary CE Primary School, Cheshunt

What Am I?

I have a thick, orange mane.
I can roar very loud.
I can pounce very far.
I live in the zoo.
I love to eat meat.
I am quite strong.
What am I?

Answer: A lion.

Papa Gyamfi Osei Afriyie (6)
Dewhurst St Mary CE Primary School, Cheshunt

What Am I?

I am found in Africa.
I have tough skin.
I am grey.
I have a horn.
I am strong.
I am bigger than a human.
What am I?

Answer: A rhino.

Sonny-Charles Lewis (6)
Dewhurst St Mary CE Primary School, Cheshunt

Sleek Fur

I have pointy ears.
I have sleek fur.
I am the king of the jungle.
In my own house, I hunt for soft toys and nibble people's toes.
I prowl around the house.
I make your lap warm.
I run in the garden.
I chase the shadows and birds.
I drink water.
What am I?

Answer: A cat.

Mabel Gleeson (5)
St Albans High School For Girls Primary School, Wheathampstead

Chain Magic

I can connect.
Some of me lives underground.
At first, I look shy, then I'm friendly.
I get thirsty.
The middle of me looks like the sun.
My colours can be brown, white, pink, green and yellow.
I can live in the wild.
What am I?

Answer: A daisy.

Emilia Calleja (5)
St Albans High School For Girls Primary School, Wheathampstead

Black And White

I look like a barcode.
I have four legs.
I look like a horse but you won't find me in stables.
I start with the letter Z.
I am the same colours as old televisions.
I have lots of stripes but you won't hear me roar.
What am I?

Answer: A zebra.

Ava Harding (6)
St Albans High School For Girls Primary School, Wheathampstead

Festival Special

I come in different sizes.
You can find me in town and at home.
But you only see me at a special time.
I have dazzling things on me.
I always have a star on top of me.
Everyone likes the things under me.
What am I?

Answer: A Christmas tree.

Melissa Wang (6)
St Albans High School For Girls Primary School, Wheathampstead

Family Fun!

Find me at the edge of the shimmering shore.
Play with me, build more and more.
Come and see my golden glow.
See how I feel between your toes.
Come and see me all year round.
Find me lying on the ground.
What am I?

Answer: Sand.

Diya Thusu (5)
St Albans High School For Girls Primary School, Wheathampstead

What Am I?

I have long ears.
I am fluffy.
I love eating carrots.
I like hopping around.
I have two sharp teeth.
I live wild in fields or sometimes kept as a pet.
You can also call me a bunny.
What am I?

Answer: A rabbit.

Marie Elena Zu Dohna (6)
St Albans High School For Girls Primary School, Wheathampstead

Two Legs

I have two legs.
I cannot walk.
I have no feet.
I cannot stand up on my own.
I can keep you warm.
I come in lots of different colours.
You can wear me.
What am I?

Answer: A pair of trousers.

Natasha Gilbert (5)
St Albans High School For Girls Primary School, Wheathampstead

Super Listener

I can hear clocks ticking from very far away.
My teeth are very pointy.
I am red and white.
I live in a burrow.
I sleep in the daytime.
I hunt for rabbits.
What am I?

Answer: A fox.

Aarya Vimal Raval (6)
St Albans High School For Girls Primary School, Wheathampstead

The Shiny And Pointy Helper

I am pointy and sharp.
I am shiny silver.
I am very thin.
I have an eye but I can't see.
I fix clothes.
I stitch but I am not a doctor.
What am I?

Answer: A sewing needle.

Anna Lucia Gonzalez (5)
St Albans High School For Girls Primary School, Wheathampstead

Beauty

I like to jump fences.
I have four legs.
I come in many sizes.
I like oats for my breakfast.
I sleep in a cosy stable.
People enjoy riding me.
What am I?

Answer: A horse.

Sarah Elizabeth Hallas (6)
St Albans High School For Girls Primary School, Wheathampstead

Eye Wonder

I am colourful.
I have feathers.
I have lots of eyes.
I like to dance.
You can see me in Whipsnade Zoo.
I am from Africa and Asia.
What am I?

Answer: A peacock.

Lara Ghosh (5)
St Albans High School For Girls Primary School, Wheathampstead

Postman

I am sticky on one side.
I travel a lot.
I don't move.
You can buy me in WH Smith.
People collect me.
You put me in a red box.
What am I?

Answer: A stamp.

Freya Burner (6)
St Albans High School For Girls Primary School, Wheathampstead

Look High To Find Me

I am bigger than human beings.
I eat you for dinner.
As soon as I'm eating you, I think you're scrumptious.
I live up high and never come down.
I live in the windy, blue sky.
I have loads of precious things to me.
I am very disturbing.
I smell as horrible as fish guts.
I smirk when I find something to eat.
I'm very dangerous so never go near me.
What am I?

Answer: A giant.

Stanley Webb (7)
St Mary's CE Academy, Hitchin

An Endangered Animal

I have no curly fur.
I am not stripy.
I am not small.
I am tall so people can see me.
I have a long trunk to suck up water when I'm thirsty.
I could be a boy or a girl.
I am very slow at walking.
I have cute, little babies.
I don't sleep much at night.
I am scary, fierce and dangerous like a spider.
I am fat, lazy and bored.
What am I?

Answer: An elephant.

Hannah Crone (7)
St Mary's CE Academy, Hitchin

The Queen

She is a queen.
She has a throne.
When she was young, she had a coronation.
On her coronation, she was given the orb and the sceptre.
She has a museum named after her.
She had nine children and she married a prince.
She lived in a house that was on the Isle of Wight.
When she was young, her husband died.
She started to wear black.
Who is she?

Answer: Queen Victoria.

Sophie Ruby Ann Deane (7)
St Mary's CE Academy, Hitchin

What Am I?

I have two little eyes and four little legs.
I have a completely black face.
I have fur all around me.
I can't run as fast as a cheetah.
I have babies but I need to do some work first.
I am a bit small and I run a little bit fast.
My back is covered in fur and the front is not.
I have no fur on my front but it is white there.
What am I?

Answer: A sheep.

Jonathan Saunders (6)
St Mary's CE Academy, Hitchin

A Yummy Treat

I can be a cake flavour.
You can have me sloppy or solid.
I am as brown as soil or as white as paper.
I can be an ice cream flavour with a brown tail sticking out.
Some people love me as a treat.
My house is a dark wrapper.
I'm normally square or rectangular but sometimes triangular.
You tear my skin and eat me.
What am I?

Answer: Chocolate.

Lucas Hall-Watts (7)
St Mary's CE Academy, Hitchin

A Sunny Person!

I'm really kind.
I'm really helpful.
I love the colour yellow.
I have light orange hair and wear bunches.
I'm in a TV program and books.
I like to tie my hair up with a red, beautiful hairband.
I have lots of good and bad friends.
I go mostly everywhere in the world.
Who am I?

Answer: *Little Miss Sunshine.*

Isla Lyons (7)
St Mary's CE Academy, Hitchin

Beautiful Isla

I go to Brownies, that is fun.
I am friends with Hannah and Ellie, they like playing schools.
I am in St. Mary's Academy, in year two.
I am the second oldest in the class, that is nice.
I am a good friend with everybody that is kind.
I am wonderful at work and I make my work pretty.
Who am I?

Answer: Isla.

Phoeby Drew (6)
St Mary's CE Academy, Hitchin

The Greatest Teacher!

I am a girl.
I have brown, curly hair.
I have some juicy, red lipstick.
I have emerald-green eyes.
I work in a classroom with thirty children
It is a happy classroom.
I love to do exciting assemblies with my amazing class.
I like to do all sorts of things.
Who am I?

Answer: Miss Wellch.

Sarah Danila (6)
St Mary's CE Academy, Hitchin

The Web

I have eight black, dangling legs like an octopus.
I have black skin like a deep, dark cave.
I have sticky webs like a daddy long legs.
I have very, very good eyesight like a crocodile.
I have been restful all day like my mum.
I have long, sharp legs like a lion.
What am I?

Answer: A spider.

Jessica Luisa Terriss (7)
St Mary's CE Academy, Hitchin

A Fast Animal

I have big, yellow eyes that glow in the dark.
I can see far away with my glowing eyes.
I live in the wonderful forest of Asia.
You can find me in zoos all over England.
I can sprint fast.
I like to roll in the zoo.
I am orange.
What am I?

Answer: A tiger.

Coen Chan (7)
St Mary's CE Academy, Hitchin

Slippery Liquid

I can be any colour.
I am a type of runny liquid.
You can put me on paper.
I have a black and white top.
You can mix me together.
I can be bright and dark colours.
You often use me on wood.
I might be in your room right now.
What am I?

Answer: Paint.

Freddie Thomas Martin (7)
St Mary's CE Academy, Hitchin

Who Am I?

I am pretty and I have brown hair.
I have two red hairclips.
I have a black and blue spotty hair bobble.
I am a girl with pretty hair clips.
I am very nice and lovely.
I am clever and sweet.
I am restful.
Who am I?

Answer: My friend, Isla.

Zeeva Turner (7)
St Mary's CE Academy, Hitchin

A Gentle Creature

I am very gentle.
I have a patterned shell.
I swim in the sparkly ocean.
I eat seaweed.
I have a family just like me.
My skin is green.
I get eaten by birds.
I walk on the beach and have a little wander.
What am I?

Answer: A turtle.

Phoebe Eliza Hooper (7)
St Mary's CE Academy, Hitchin

The Juicy Squeezer

They are as round as a ball.
They are as juicy as a pink pig.
You can buy them at the supermarket.
They go in the fridge.
They are as cold as a dream.
They are very delicious to eat.
They can be purple.
What are they?

Answer: Grapes.

Bryher Goodluck (6)
St Mary's CE Academy, Hitchin

A Swinging Animal

I have brown fur.
I have silky, wet skin.
I swing on branches.
I eat fruit and vegetables.
I eat apricots and melons.
I have a wild wife and a wild baby.
I am a boy and I like to play in the forest.
What am I?

Answer: A monkey.

Ellie Newman (6)
St Mary's CE Academy, Hitchin

Green And Mean

It is short and full.
It can be spiky and dangerous.
It can be flowery and beautiful.
It can be a shelter for small animals.
You can find it on the edge of a field.
It never moves but waves in the breeze.
What is it?

Answer: A bush.

Finley Horton (6)
St Mary's CE Academy, Hitchin

A Royal Ruler

It lives with an important person.
It lives in a big tower.
It is a beautiful gem keeper.
It is a heavy hat.
The important person is a gem wearer.
It is for a great ruler.
It has shiny, gold skin.
What is it?

Answer: A crown.

London-Grace Isabella Maria Rodrigues de Souza (6)
St Mary's CE Academy, Hitchin

The Fluffy Animal

It has ginger and brown stripes.
You can't get it in any shop but a pet shop.
It can go anywhere day or night.
It has a soft body.
It has pointy ears.
It has black whiskers.
It loves its owners.
What is it?

Answer: A cat.

Isabelle Marsh (6)
St Mary's CE Academy, Hitchin

Old Animal

I have a dark orange body with lots of stripes.
I have a huge, long tail.
I am big and strong.
I lived a long time ago.
I am very scary, so if you see me, run away.
I'm a bit like a monster.
What am I?

Answer: A dinosaur.

Jamie Thompson (7)
St Mary's CE Academy, Hitchin

The Scrumptious Food

I have a juicy cherry on the top.
You can make me in all different shapes and sizes.
I am delicious to eat.
You can get me from a bakery.
I am very, very bouncy.
I am colourful on the top.
What am I?

Answer: A cake.

Grace Kelly (7)
St Mary's CE Academy, Hitchin

My Magic

It's magical.
It's got patterns.
It's an object, not a living thing.
It has a carved stand with the same patterns.
It's very long and pointy.
It can snap.
What is it?

Answer: Hermione's wand.

Freya Jane Shapland (7)
St Mary's CE Academy, Hitchin

A Fast Animal

I'm very fast and spotty.
I have a team called Arsenal who sponsor me.
I live in the deep, dark jungle.
I have yellow fur.
I have sharp, razor teeth.
I have a curly tail.
What am I?

Answer: A puma.

Miles O'Brien (7)
St Mary's CE Academy, Hitchin

What Am I?

I'm round.
I fall off trees in midsummer.
I'm very popular.
You may find me in a shop.
I will rot if you don't put me in the fridge.
I am very, very sweet.
What am I?

Answer: An apple.

Felix Weston (6)
St Mary's CE Academy, Hitchin

Oxygen Giver

It has a small trunk.
It has green leaves.
Some are small and some are big.
It can blow in the breeze.
It can grow fruit.
It loses its leaves.
It gathers blossom.
What is it?

Answer: A tree.

Sid White (6)
St Mary's CE Academy, Hitchin

Slimy Jumper

I live in a cage in a house.
I come in many colours.
I can lick my eyes with my long tongue.
I can curl my long, delicate tail.
I can climb walls with my sticky feet.
What am I?

Answer: A gecko.

Toby Matthew Pearce (6)
St Mary's CE Academy, Hitchin

What Is It?

It may be shiny.
It can be seen in the dark.
It is stripy and furry.
It has babies called cubs.
It hunts to eat.
It could attack you.
What is it?

Answer: A snowy tiger.

Logan Hall (7)
St Mary's CE Academy, Hitchin

What Am I?

I can pick up apples.
I have a long trunk.
I can live in the jungle.
I eat juicy leaves.
I have a short tail.
I have chunky legs.
What am I?

Answer: An elephant.

James Lyon (6)
St Mary's CE Academy, Hitchin

What Am I?

I slither slowly.
I fall out of trees.
I have a poisonous bite.
I'm a carnivore.
I am black like space.
I live in logs.
What am I?

Answer: A cobra.

Morgan John Geary (7)
St Mary's CE Academy, Hitchin

Animals

I'm endangered.
I'm cute.
My favourite food is bamboo.
I live in the deep forests of China.
I have a little tail.
What am I?

Answer: A panda.

William Whybrow (6)
St Mary's CE Academy, Hitchin

The Riddle Riddler

I run as fast as lightning.
I have silky, soft fur.
I'm as fast as a motorbike.
I love running and jumping in the grass.
What am I?

Answer: A cheetah.

Blue Bartlett (7)
St Mary's CE Academy, Hitchin

A Field Liver

A powerful jumper.
A straw eater.
A fast runner.
A grass eater.
An apple eater.
A carrot eater.
A nice rider.
What am I?

Answer: A horse.

Peyton Jean Day (7)
St Mary's CE Academy, Hitchin

Am I Tasty?

I have a white coat.
You might get messy if you touch me.
I am not a fruit or vegetable.
You might see me in a cookbook.
What am I?

Answer: A cupcake.

Oliver Ibbotson (7)
St Mary's CE Academy, Hitchin

Miles

A good walker.
A good sleeper.
A walk lover.
A lover.
A hair shaver.
A sniffer.
A lone walker.
What am I?

Answer: A puppy.

Eliana Miles (6)
St Mary's CE Academy, Hitchin

What Am I?

A great climbing animal.
A loving animal.
A cute animal.
A night hungry animal.
A fun play-fighter.
What am I?

Answer: A panda.

Alfie Witherington (6)
St Mary's CE Academy, Hitchin

Who Am I?

A wealth catcher.
A code breaker.
A poor person to a rich person.
A bank user.
A stripy disguiser.
Who am I?

Answer: A robber.

Max Harvey (6)
St Mary's CE Academy, Hitchin

Who Am I?

I am a good friend.
I am a person who joins their capital letters up.
I like playing cops and robbers.
Who am I?

Answer: Milo.

Liam Maw (7)
St Mary's CE Academy, Hitchin

What Am I?

I'm a baby, spotty and brown.
I have black and yellow fur.
I have grey spots and dark yellow.
What am I?

Answer: A hyena.

Connor Crook (6)
St Mary's CE Academy, Hitchin

Growing Time

I sleep deep in the ground.
I grow from a bulb.
I am the national flower of Wales.
I am named after a Greek myth.
I can be as yellow as the sun, as orange as a carrot, pink or lime.
I have a trumpet.
I bloom at the beginning of spring.
I can grow in the snow.
I am the flower of March.
What am I?

Answer: A daffodil.

Elysia Kyriacou
Trent CE Primary School, Cockfosters

Great Power

I have a beautiful, colourful horn.
I have a long mane like a rainbow in the sky.
When I appear, you can feel that I'm here.
I can fly high in the sky like a beautiful bird.
You can be amazed by my magical skills.
You can ride on me and we'll dash through the sky quickly.
What am I?

Answer: A unicorn.

Paraskevi Angeli (6)
Trent CE Primary School, Cockfosters

Snow Storm

I am not a living thing for I am made of snow.
I have a carrot nose.
I have arms made out of sticks.
I have three buttons on my tummy.
I have a fluffy hat.
Matched with a stripy scarf.
Two shiny eyes and a huge smile.
What am I?

Answer: A snowman.

Greatwin Anyanwu (6)
Trent CE Primary School, Cockfosters

Build Me!

I can be any colour you want.
I can be small and sometimes big.
I have tiny circles on top of me.
I come in different kinds of shapes.
I can be made into any structure you want.
I am the most popular toy in England.
What am I?

Answer: Lego.

Ben Jones (7)
Trent CE Primary School, Cockfosters

Fun Time!

Lots of people are sunbathing and playing in me.
No one is working, everyone is having fun.
I am very hot.
You can wear shorts when I am here.
When I'm around, it's nice to eat ice cream.
I relax a lot.
What am I?

Answer: Summer.

Isabella Fitzgerald (6)
Trent CE Primary School, Cockfosters

Paws And Play!

I am very cuddly and furry.
I come in all shapes and colours.
I can be small or big.
When I am happy, I wag my tail.
I have four legs.
I can't talk but I bark.
What am I?

Answer: A dog.

Zoe Koureas (6)
Trent CE Primary School, Cockfosters

Cool Creature

I am the largest land carnivore.
I have white, thick fur.
The tip of my nose is black.
I have an incredible sense of smell.
I like eating ringed seals.
What am I?

Answer: A polar bear.

Christopher Jacovou (7)
Trent CE Primary School, Cockfosters

Monkey Riddle

I'm brown.
I live in a tree.
I swing in the trees.
I love bananas and fruit a lot.
What am I?

Answer: A monkey.

Natasha Anna Kyriacou (7)
Trent CE Primary School, Cockfosters

Furry And Fluffy

I'm so furry and fluffy.
I'm like a pillow for bedtime.
I have colourful fur.
I can be dark and not all colourful.
I move with my sharp claws and smelly paws.
I have very sharp claws so when people annoy me, I can scratch them.
Sometimes, they have pink ears.
I'm small but if I eat too much food, I can get big.
I eat pet biscuits and pet wet food.
Sometimes, I have a red nose.
I have tiny eyes.
What am I?

Answer: A cat.

Madeline Valentine (7)
Warren Dell Primary School, South Oxhey

No Feet, But Wheels

I have three rockets that make a triangle.
I have a black nose at the front.
I have two pairs of wings with no sharp end.
You might find me in a plane museum with space stuff.
I am built in America.
I have three wheels that come inside.
I have five windows at the front.
I have an open bit.
What am I?

Answer: A space shuttle.

Alex Webster (7)
Warren Dell Primary School, South Oxhey

Skinny, Short But Fast

I climb tall trees.
I have long, shiny claws.
If I ran away, you would never catch me.
I am quite tiny and skinny.
I like eating smaller animals.
My legs are short, skinny and bony.
I have a spotty pattern like a leopard.
I don't have teeth, only gums.
What am I?

Answer: A leopard gecko.

Aiva Lardner (7)
Warren Dell Primary School, South Oxhey

Eat Meat, Fast Feet

I love to eat meat.
I have fast feet and two legs.
I have two hands.
I live in Africa.
You might find me in dry, open grasslands.
You see me run.
Balls are my favourite game to play.
Beware, because I'm fierce.
I'm in the cat family.
What am I?

Answer: A cheetah.

Alfie Quidder-Hart (7)
Warren Dell Primary School, South Oxhey

Take Off And Fly Away!

I am teeny tiny.
I am magic.
I have wings.
I like to sprinkle.
I live in a mushroom city.
I like to fly.
What am I?

Answer: A fairy.

Jessica Burman (6)
Warren Dell Primary School, South Oxhey

YoungWriters
Est.1991

YOUNG WRITERS INFORMATION

We hope you have enjoyed reading this book – and that you will continue to in the coming years.

If you're a young writer who enjoys reading and creative writing, or the parent of an enthusiastic poet or story writer, do visit our website **www.youngwriters.co.uk**. Here you will find free competitions, workshops and games, as well as recommended reads, a poetry glossary and our blog.

If you would like to order further copies of this book, or any of our other titles, then please give us a call or visit **www.youngwriters.co.uk**.

Young Writers
Remus House
Coltsfoot Drive
Peterborough
PE2 9BF
(01733) 890066
info@youngwriters.co.uk